Rock O

This book belongs to

Portesham CE VA Primary School

Alex taps a tin can with a stick.
Tap. Tap.

She wants a better sound.
She slips a sock on
the end of the stick.
That's better.

dum
dee
dum

My drum rocks!

2

You can beat a drum:

hard and loud

soft and low

slow

quick

Josh bangs two pot lids.
Clash! Bash! Crash!

He wants a better sound.
He slides the lids across
each other.

Sh! Clash!

My lids rock!

4

Kate shakes some peas in a box.
Pitter-patter. Pitter-patter.

She shakes some shells in a sock.
She likes that better.

My shells rock!

clatter-smatter

Denzil hooks string round a box.
He plucks the wire.
It sounds just right. It sounds like the rain.

My box rocks!

drip-**drop**
drip-**drop**

Vicky blows into a tube.
Long. Short. Short. Long.
The tube squeaks and squeals.
It is singing a song.

Shane pats his legs.
He slaps his arms.

He claps his hands and rubs his chest.

clap, clap, shh

Alex starts to tap her drum.
They all start to play to the beat.

The beat might get faster or louder
or slower or softer.
They all copy the drum beat.

Faster, louder, slower, softer.

Sh! **Clash!**

clatter-
smatter

dum
dee
dum

They are all making their own sounds to the beat. They all rock!

slip, slap

drip-**drop**
drip-**drop**

wee-waa
wee-waa

clap, clap, shh

Rock out!

tin can, stick and sock

pot lids

shells in a sock

14

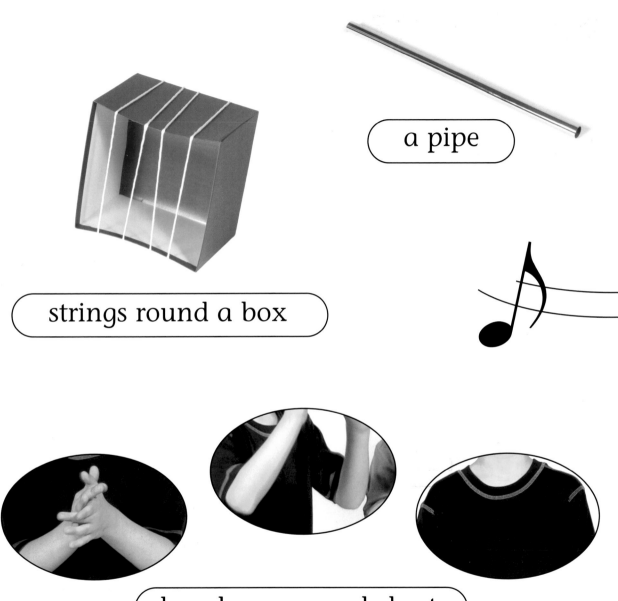

a pipe

strings round a box

hands, arms and chest

Ideas for reading

Learning objectives: Use phonological knowledge to work out, predict and check the meanings of unfamiliar words and to make sense of what they read; Blend phonemes for reading.

Curriculum links: Music: Exploring pulse and rhythm; Exploring instruments and symbols; Science: Making different sounds.

Focus phonemes: i-e (like, slides, wire), u-e (tube), ea (beat, squeaks, squeals), igh (right, might), ow (low, slow)

Fast words: she, wants, the, of, two, some, into, he, they, their

Word count: 263

Getting started

- Write the words that include the focus phonemes *i-e, u-e, ea, igh* and *ow* on a small whiteboard and ask the children to fast-read them, blending aloud if they need to. Do these words give the children any clues about what will happen in the story?

- Before introducing the book, talk about the phrase *My drum rocks* and ask the children to explain what this kind of expression means to them. Ask them to substitute other words for drum, e.g. *My mum rocks.*

- Reveal the book's cover from the right side, showing one musician at a time. Ask the children to say what sounds each instrument might make. Do they notice that the instruments are home made?

Reading and responding

- Give the children copies of the book to read independently.

- Check that the children are blending the words where necessary and draw their attention to the text in bold, in the speech bubbles and in the captions. Highlight the different expression used for each of these.

- Check that the children are phrasing sentences correctly and pausing at full stops for the intended effect, e.g. after *Pitter-patter* on p5.

- When children have reached p9, ask: *What is different about Shane's instrument?*